Waldman House Press, Inc.
525 North Third Street
Minneapolis, Minnesota 55401

A is for Adult

An Alphabet Book For Grown-Ups

Written and illustrated by
Warren Hanson

Waldman House Press • Minneapolis

A is for Adult. I've got to Adjust

To being midway between Ashes and dust.

I'm trapped here in midlife, that period when

I feel like I'm eighty and wish I were ten.

B is for Barely, a word that refers

To the trials we face as adulthood occurs.

I Barely have hair, Barely can touch my toes,

And I Barely, just Barely, fit into my clothes.

C is for Cash, but I'm in arrears.

My money is magic — it just disappears!

They say money talks, and sometimes even sings!

But my money flies away, like it has wings!

D is for every Deduction I claim

In trying to win at the income tax game.

If Shakespeare wrote fiction like this, you'd applaud it.

When I write it, I get paid back with an audit.

E is for Easy, like things used to be,

Like riding a bike, or like climbing a tree.

How did that kind of activity end?

Didn't my Elbows and knees used to bend?

F is for Fake it. I've gotten quite good!

Like when the mechanic points under the hood

And says that my Flange rockers should be retooled.

I say, "Yeah, I thought so." I've sure got him Fooled!

G is the letter for Get Up and Go,

That unbridled energy I used to know.

But the years have done something I could not prevent —

My Get Up and Go just Got Up and Went.

H is the Hurry that I'm always in.

Although all this rushing can make my Head spin,

If life would slow down, I would just start to worry.

I'd say more about this, but I'm in a Hurry.

I is for whole life and term life Insurance,

Which means that I'm betting against my endurance.

If I'm understanding the plan that I'm in,

The earlier I die, the more that I win.

J is for Jury, and I'm proud to serve,

To mete out the Justice that people deserve.

But to make sure my Judgment's not tainted by leaks,

I end up sequestered with strangers for weeks.

K is a measure of how far you run.

Some of my peers do this torture for fun!

If you think that I'm going to do this with you,

Then K is for Kill me, which is what it would do.

L is for Literature, which this isn't.

But most books I've seen are so Long and unpleasant.

What I Love to read, all curled up in pajamas,

Are those color brochures from the balmy Bahamas.

M is for Mortgage, and I think it's scary
'Cause it shares the same root as the word "Mortuary."

Among all my nightmares, this one is the worst:
Which of the two of them will be paid first?

N is for Naked. It used to be passion

That made me throw off all the trappings of fashion.

But these days I notice, when I am undressing,

The body I see in the mirror's depressing!

O is for Over, like "Over the hill."

The years are victorious Over the will.

But, just in case you feel too young to relate,

Try this on for size: O is for Overweight.

P is the Paycheck that's already small

Before they take taxes, insurance and all.

Yet the time will soon come, I should hasten to mention,

When I'll wish they had taken <u>more</u> out … for my Pension.

Q is for Question. Way back in my youth
I knew all the answers, was sure of the truth.

But these days, when asked if I'll share a suggestion,
Most often my answer is, "What was the Question?"

R is the music, that great Rock 'n' Roll,

Which was hard on the hearing, but good for the soul.

Now that I'm older, when I twist and shout,

It usually means that my back has gone out.

S is for Stock. I'm a lousy investor.

I should have devoted at least a semester

To learning how I can retire in the sun.

My interest is growing in mutual fun.

T is for Taxes, and I live in Terror

That I will make some arithmetical error

In one of the boxes on my Form 1040

Which gives me new roommates named Knuckles & Shorty.

U is for Used to. I Used to be thin,

Used to stay up past ten, Used to have just one chin.

Reminiscing won't bring back my youth — not one bit.

Age happens, but I just can't get Used to it.

V is the Virtue of Vintage Vitality,

And Vitamins in Volume to Vanquish mortality.

Vexed by aches and by pains, and by Varicose Veins,

I'm Victorious over Virus's Virulent strains.

W stands for the Wonderful Weekend.

Lately a Whole Week of Work leaves me Weakened.

I need two days off so that I can feel stronger.

I only Wish, somehow, Weekends Would be longer.

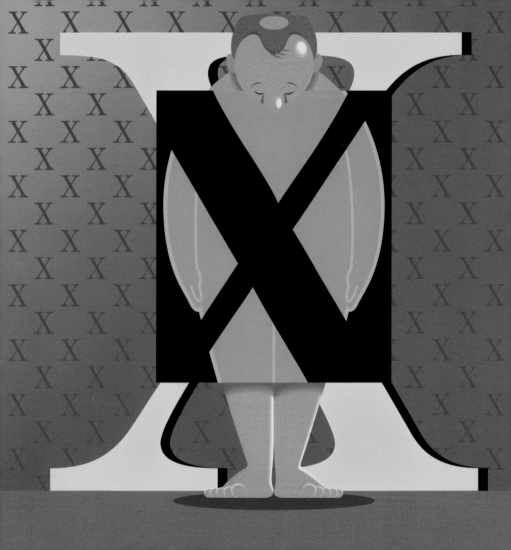

X is for X-ray, and I've had my share.

Maybe that's why I am losing my hair!

When I was young, X-rays were quite unremarkable.

Now I've had so many, I'm glow-in-the-darkable.

Y is for Yesterday, when I was Young,

Before all my nerves were completely unstrung.

I'm as nervous as the well-known proverbial cat.

I'd love to calm down, but I … WHAT WAS THAT?!

Z is for Zipper, a wondrous invention!

Though I doubt it was the inventor's intention

That I be embarrassed to put on my pants.

Last week I could Zip them. This week? Not a chance!

Now that you know the Adult ABC's,

I beg you for some of your sympathy, please?

Time marches on, there's not much I can do.

Yes, I'm getting older. But then, so are you!